Thriving Through Pain

"Discovering the Power of Grace Within"

by

Kristin Shipman

Copyright © 2024 Kristin Shipman

Published by Newlifepoetrylive

All rights reserved.

No part of this publication may be reproduced, distributed or transmitted in any form or by any means, including photocopying, recording or other electronic or mechanical methods, without the prior written permission of the publisher, except in the case of brief quotations, reviews and other noncommercial uses permitted by copyright law.

978-1-960245-05-2

Blue Diamond Bookhouse

Contents

Dedication v
Introduction vii

CHAPTER 1. PAIN IN THE MIRROR 1

Hope's Light 3
Silent Addiction. 5
Transforming Dreams 7
Gone away 9
Suffocating Silence 11
Frozen Time 13
Slowing down. 15

CHAPTER 2. STEPPING INTO LIGHT. 17

Made For More. 19
Thankful Moments 21
Healing words. 23
As Long as 25
Press On 27
Pep Talk for the Soul 29
Joy's Anchor. 31
Purpose Reborn. 33
Waiting to Run 35

CHAPTER 3. A DISCOVERY MADE 37
Higher *39*
The Moment life changed. *41*
Joy's Overflow *43*
Another Day *45*
Thrive *47*
Pain Into Purpose *49*
What I AM. *51*
Everlasting Love *53*
A Pen's Crown. *55*
A New Sound *57*
About the Author *61*

Dedication

This book is dedicated to my Lord and Savior Jesus, whom pulled me from a place of surviving and taught me how to thrive. To Michael, who has stood by my side and became inspiration to many of these poems and to the many amazing mentors I've had in my life the past 5 years. To my children and family who have watched me transform into the woman I am today. I am grateful for all of you. This book is a seed into the advancement for hearts to be reconciled to the kingdom.

Introduction

Introducing "Thriving Through Pain": a collection of poems that will inspire and empower you to find strength and beauty amidst life's toughest trials. In this heartfelt anthology, the author delves deep into the human experience, inviting readers to explore their own identity, faith, and endurance. Through poignant verses and uplifting messages, these poems serve as a guiding light, reminding us that our worth is not defined by the challenges we face, but by the resilience and grace with which we rise above them. Join us on this transformative journey and discover how pain can be transformed into a powerful catalyst for growth. "Thriving Through Pain" is a testament to the inherent strength within us all, and a reminder that even in the darkest moments, we have the power to emerge as masterpieces in the eyes of God.

Chapter 1
Pain in the Mirror

Hope's Light

There are days where I don't see up from down
Where the trees don't look to bloom
Where it's too crowded in a room
My smile begins to turn to a frown
There are days when heaviness entraps my mind
Thoughts of lies and deception unkind
Only but for a moment before light again takes over
It's a wonder
How God's Word saves a soul from darkness,
piercing through time and space like a surgical knife to the heart,
the root of who we are and who we are to become
Shaking us back to Christ realities, cheerleading us on through embraced Truth
By the seeds of life sown into us
By the darkness that has come into the light in obedience of its own
It's right and it's so bright
It pierces through any night
Like the star in Bethlehem that wise men once knew
Hearts renewed
Here today, the same as always available just for you.

Silent Addiction

There's an addiction- a friction
Of words left untold
Break out from the old told
Step out, be the new mold

You may just discover
Something new and grand
A gift, a talent or a dream
A diamond more precious than gold

Be bold, I know that you can!
Arise from that old dead man inside
There is too much beautiful in you
The world needs you just do not hide

Transforming Dreams

Wrangled in the wreckage of a dream shut down
Seems all you know now is to keep a frown
What if you began again and dreamt brand new
Perhaps it would refresh you like a mornings dew

A world of fantasies a place free to dream
Setbacks make a heart want to yell and scream
For every circumstance a lesson to be learned
For every victory a defeat to be burned

Times and seasons they come for all
You may run or you may begin to fall
Still yet you will get the choice to choose
Will you win or will you make a choice to lose?

Gone away

Like a knife that never stops cutting
So are triggers of the heart
When you are not here with me
It should have been from the start

Beating thinking about where you might be
Protect him Lord where I don't see
Here alone in my bedroom
I'm down here begging on my knees

Suffocating Silence

Tick tock hands on a clock
Boom boom goes my heart beating
Pitter patter the raindrops fall
Drip drop as tears begin to fall

His love was so pure
His words so divine
Now where has he gone
With his heart carrying mine

I pray that he's safe
I trust God that he is okay
Yet in my spirit Im feeling
Like our future now has delay

It's not just at all
It's not right to say the least
A soldier to return home
A beast to now defeat

Bring him home safely Lord
I know what you've shown me
The dreams that we share
My heart a door and he holds the key

Frozen Time

I'm Frozen in time
I guess it's time to rhyme
I don't know what to write
Everything is out of sight
But it feels so right
In the darkness to be the light
To pull from deep within
To see yourself to grin
What was is not who you are
No matter what you have seen from afar
Today in this moment you decide
Where to go and how you want to ride

Slowing down

So tired the eyes cannot help but weep
Your body is screaming "I just need some sleep!"
Take a deep breath exhale every weight
Trust and believe tomorrow will be great

One day has enough worries of its own
There's more treasure in you yet to be known
Keep pressing in you know that you can
Look deep within go ahead take that scan

There you will see treasures unfold
More precious than silver, diamonds or gold
You are loved far beyond man can compare
God loves you so much he counts every hair

Take care of your vessel do not overdo
Be diligent you will discover a brand new you
One moment at a time breath in real slow
The world is waiting for you, do you know?

A mess to a message all pain to your gain
They may not know the days you felt the rain
You are stepping into your greatest of days
Surely those discoveries are prepared to amaze

Chapter Two
Stepping Into Light

Made For More

There's a flowing river
Passing along the banks of my mind
Around the rocks between the trees
It's a journey one of a kind

The sun rises each new day
As hopes and dreams guide the way
The sunset revealing transformation
Clouds billow by each a new creation

Paddling upstream eyes on the horizon
Fears being released the load begins to lighten
Make way back to shore
Come back tomorrow again once more

Thankful Moments

This fly buzzing around my head
Wishing now I was upon my bed
So much yet I need to do
Taking a pause to write something new

I count my blessings one by one
I see todays victories that I have won
Take a breath everything is okay
My Fathers love always makes a way

The kids now sleeping in their beds
I give them a kiss upon their heads
Protect them Father as they sleep
Do not let their hearts to weep

I take my mirror and behold me there
Sitting down in my rocking chair
I took the steps I pressed on through
Seeing today how my garden grew

The past behind looking now forward
Time with Jesus just what love ordered
Thank you Lord I'm a grateful heart
Tomorrow with you is a brand new start.

Healing words

Pen on paper potential is waiting
A heart so deep keep on creating
The clock keeps ticking "tick tock"
Your spirit says "let's rock!"

One word , then two and then one more
What are all of these words even for?
Could it be the start of an open door?
Or passion for a life of even more?

Take a break for a smile
Tell your troubled heart it's been awhile
Pain and strife cut deep like a knife
Keep up joy it strengthens your life

So write one more word sow one more tear
Think another thought release every fear
A winning battle is now being fought
This inner growth it cannot be bought

As Long as

As long as you are far away..
I'll send a kiss upon the wind.
Long as I hear your heart beating…
I'll play to the beat of our song.
As long as you strum a melody…
You will always find a way to find me.
As long as I see the truth in your eyes…
My love will always be yours.
As long as you embrace me …
You will never hunger for my touch.
As long as you invest your time into us..
Your wealth will overflow.
Long as you pray for me and our family
Your happiness grows in fertile ground.
Long as the stars shine in the sky …
I will stand by you.
Long as the sun goes over the horizon..
I will always be with you.

As Long as

Press On

God loves me… unconditionally
He trusts me with His word.
I choose to activate that Light in me.
I will speak boldly with my sword.

No pain or lie can hold me down
No problem, sickness or broken crown
For the truth that I have planted inside
My Father in Him I know that I reside

Heavens angels anxiously awaiting
Anticipating my command
Rising tall I shall continue
Taking up my stand!

Pep Talk for the Soul

Here and there so many voices and stares
I'll keep on pushing I know my Father cares
I search for truth and lies knock on my door
Whatever it takes even prostrate on the floor

I know what to do
to create my heart anew
Back to the drawing board
Time to get out my sword

Life gets hard when you need to redirect
You have to choose what you will select
Disappointment comes or hope begins to drown
Hold tight beloved, get up and straighten your crown

Joy's Anchor

In the midst of times we are waiting
It can be so very clear
That every heavy weight of this world
Can be lifted far from here

And when your heart is resting
In the loving arms you Know
Jesus carries the burden
When it's joy that you sow

This moment is but temporary
So there is no reason to fear
Just renew your mind in His truth
And your heart will sing my dear

There is a world that is hurting
But there's kingdom flourishing too
So let your mind stay fixed upon
The one whose running for you

Jesus
The anchor of my soul
Oh how I love you
I'm just letting you know

Now to all my friends who are listening
To every heart be sad or glad
Father I ask that you'd touch them
Let them grab their notepad

Today please bring them through
To the hope they are in Christ
To every promise and every word that
Your peace and love renews

The schemes of the enemy are no match
For your spirit is a wonder; it's quite a catch
Renew your mind cast away every care
Dig deeper into Gods love if you dare

Believe to know your Fathers heart
He will once again give you a fresh new start
Treasures to behold and gifts to ignite
The greater One inside won't give up the fight

Decree, declare and stand tall once again
Look into His eyes His truth lifts up your chin
Let His oil drip down upon your skin
You are His beloved; born to triumph and WIN!

Purpose Reborn

I've lost intentionality
Hope deferred has become my reality
I know I shouldn't feel this way
I just cannot get moving on with my day

Get it back
Stab it in the back with purpose
Baby steps heavy as a stone
I need to get back up onto that throne

Waiting to Run

Buried in the grainy sand real deep
Like a baby turtle securely fast asleep
Waiting for the bright sun to shine
Seeking to come out at just the right time

The waves of life come in and go out
Just as well does hope and doubt
There is a season for everything
What a joy passions movement can bring

So rest your head little one
Your waiting will soon be done
Then you're journey will have begun
As you take those steps and begin to run

Chapter Three
A Discovery Made

Higher

My feet on the ground I go higher
My heart positioned right I go higher

This tempest inside, the waves growing
Slowing
To the peaceful rivers within
A new place to again begin

Attitude checked I go higher
Dreams building I go higher
My soul sings like a choir
Hands lifted to go higher
Made from the clay and the mire
I am His only desire

The Moment life changed

The wheels turned round real fast
As praise was on her lips
Another day, another opportunity
The sun kissing her cheeks
As she looked in her rear view mirror one last time
At the woman she once was before this rhyme
Looking ahead at the dreams before her coming into view; all brand new

Just as moments come and go
Traffic halted she didn't know
The brakes froze up no stopping
The course of the day changed
Her body began rocking

Her joy moment turned to tears
No time to think about all of her years

The airbag deployed
SMASH!
The other drivers became very annoyed
At the delay now being viewed before them

A choice to control fear or embrace life
She is a warrior not a woman of strife
Not a thought she moved from the wreckage and then

Like an angels embrace
No disgrace just peace; a release
As she sat and breathed heavily
She could see her king there readily
Holding out his hand
Then she knew that she had
This moment in her control
The car took its toll
The enemy lost that's how she rolls
A life's purpose kept protected
From the wreckage of the world's ways
Resurrection power quickened
She rose again with her strong tower
Gentle as a dove or like an opened flower
Hands lifted high it wasn't time to say goodbye
She dusted off her clothes

She composed her thoughts and spoke to her soul
She closed her eyes and beheld her king again
A thankful heart for another start
With heightened perspective of purpose once more
Only God knows what He yet has in store
A moment that changed a life

Joy's Overflow

Joys Overflow hung up the phone
His love to her has become well known
The wrenching pain in her stomach grew
What was this? Something new
Beginning as a tempest storm
This pain was far from the norm

Sirens rang
At the door there was a BANG!
Crippled over on the floor
Where Joy had rested her faith now being tested
They checked her pulse
They loaded her up

Pain wrenching, clenching on tight
She wasn't about to give up this fight!
She knew her way, she knew her rights
Singing through the tears
From all the prepared years
Her nature began to neutralize
Knowing already she had won the prize

Her savior's embrace
This was an easy race
Healed delivered whole and brand new
Very few had known all that she had gone through
Step by step one word released after another
She thought of all her sisters and brothers

The morphine went in "drip drip"
The pain stabbed harder deep breaths
Holding fast heart beating
Eyes welled up and weeping
What was happening

Her Choice to reign
In her domain
She spoke out louder
This time in praise!
Amazed
Her future seen
Living backwards from her dreams
Into the seams of where her heart grows
Testimony revealed
Healed
Back into Joys Overflow

Another Day

Another day to love you, another day to win
May the sun shine upon your face
May God wrap you in His warm embrace
As I behold Him I too see you
I thank Him for all you say and do
We get to build each day brand new
With all I become and all I am, I love you

Thrive

Awaken a drive so alive inside
A place to dwell and abide
By the pictures that I get to see
There could never be a better me

A poem for a poet
A painting for an artist
A king for a Queen
With God we can do Amazing things

So stand up against all odds
Release the greater within
There are unlimited seeds within you
Let the journey begin!

-Kristin Shipman & Pierre Ingram

Pain Into Purpose

I embrace the pain of my past
It didn't last
I no longer live there
The shame and guilt that tried to swallow me up
It had me stuck up in chains, no gains.
In the midst of the waves they no longer have me bound
I've been found
I was brought out of the pit and rediscovered
Purpose from the pain
It was gain
In my new mindset I remain
I'm no longer the same

I beheld that girl in the mirror today
I told her how brave and courageous she was
To embrace the pain
The despair she wore on her face I wiped away
She became so brave she conquered the waves
It's a new day!
His mercies are new to stay
Now her voice can be heard to guide the way
To others who have not embraced the pain
Into better days
Where truth remains

In this life that's stretched beyond our yesterdays; now embrace the change

I grabbed her hand and pulled her through the door of grace into a new space

To embrace

The dawning of a new day, a brighter shine, a new way to give glory

A new story

Purpose in the pain

What I AM

I Am the heart that loves deeply

I Am a song that sings sweetly

I Am passionately pursuing my dreams

I Am fire bursting at the seams

I Am sweet fragrance by my praise

I Am yielded to His ways

I Am faithful to remain humble

I Am not made to struggle

I Am teachable

I Am nearly always reachable

I Am His hope

I Am a kaleidoscope

I Am forgiven

I Am forever driven

I Am never alone

I Am seated on His throne

I Am that which I say I am

Everlasting Love

In a world where beauty thrives,
Where the heart with passion flies,
There exists an ethereal flame,
With a power no tongue can name.
Love, the force that binds us all,
In its embrace, we stand tall.
Through the ages, it does endure,
Pure and precious, forevermore.
Love is the gentle touch of grace,
That brings a smile to every face.
It heals the wounds that scar the soul,
Makes us feel complete and whole.
Love, the language of the heart,
With it, we find our truest part.
It knows no limits, knows no bounds,
In its depths, a mystery profound.
It's in the laughter and the tears,
In the presence that conquers fears.
It's the warmth in a comforting hug,
The strength that lifts, the gentle tug.
Love is a melody, sweet and serene,
That echoes in moments, unforeseen.
It paints colors across life's canvas,
Creating bonds that will never vanish.

It's the light that guides through darkest night,
A beacon of hope, shining so bright.
Love is the dance of souls entwined,
An eternal bond, so divinely designed.
So let us cherish this gift we have,
With every beat of heart, let's be brave.
For love is the essence that makes us whole,
The fire that ignites our very soul.

A Pen's Crown

In the dark of the night as a light breaks forth
A new passion ignites, a story to be told
Brighter and brighter as the sun arises
No longer does her heart wear disguises

Many let her down
As she turned those frowns upside down
Many devalued her time
As her life turned into a rhyme

She straightened her crown said "it's time to reign"
They never knew what would become of her name
Taking a pen to write on the paper
To tell the twists and turns that one day saved her.

Strength and endurance she grew and grew
Her heart was enlarged as she became brand new
And all of a sudden flame became a fire
From all of her passions, all of her desires

The dam now unlocked
Creativity began to flow
In all of her life she never knew the potential
Of what one day she would get to sow.

A New Sound

Mountains Move!
Breaking Now!
Kings shall speak!
Bold not weak!

There is a cry of revival
We are breaking from survival…
We shall Thrive!
The church, Come Alive!

The time is Now
Every evil bow!
The Light is here
And angels near

Are you ready for revival?
Are you ready for His arrival?

The bold shall stand
All across this land
There's a new sound arising
The glory will be surprising

Stand your ground!
Let Christ be found
There's a new awakening
Hearts He is straightening

In this empowering journey, Kristin Shipman navigates you through the doors of your heart to amplify areas where growth, submission, or healing may need to take place. You will experience a deeper awareness of your identity in Christ and you will be given a choice to see your inner being as in a mirror; Christ in you-the hope of glory. Get ready to discover enlightenment, wisdom and truth as you become "love expressed" to a hurting world.

About the Author

Kristin Shipman is a loyal and faithful heart sent to impact this generation, a woman that God has molded "to express His unfailing love." She carries a gift of encouragement to give hope to the world and to the body of Christ. Since her days in high school, she has taken a deep dive into Christ and transformed into a greaterawareness of God within by building a strong foundation for her faith. She is the mother of five children and two grandchildren who have been a witness of her praise through the storms and turbulence of life. A strong woman of faith and kingdom connector, she has been activated to move in miracles, signs and wonders and has seen firsthand blind eyes restored, arthritis disappear, as well as being witness to countless miracles through her spiritual covering Dr.'s Charles and Donna Ndifon through Christ Love Ministries International. She was born in Des Moines, IA and has had poems published in the International Library of Poetry. She joyfully serves alongside impactful leaders worldwide and continues to bring encouragement, unity, hope and healing to a hurting world.